FAILURE

Business
BLUNDERS

S0-BUE-811

Kristy Stark, M.A.Ed.

Publishing Credits

Rachelle Cracchiolo, M.S.Ed., *Publisher*
Conni Medina, M.A.Ed., *Managing Editor*
Nika Fabienke, Ed.D., *Series Developer*
June Kikuchi, *Content Director*
John Leach, *Assistant Editor*
Kevin Pham, *Graphic Designer*

TIME and the TIME logo are registered trademarks of TIME Inc. Used under license.

Image Credits: pp.4–5 Krista Kennell/Shutterstock; pp.6–7 Ryan Fletcher/Shutterstock; p.7 (top) Art Konovalov/Shutterstock; pp.8–9 Library of Congress [LC-DIG-det-4a27966]; pp.12–13 Jonathan Little/Alamy; p.15 (center left) Ivan Kurmyshov/Shutterstock; p.16 (bottom) SSPL/Getty Images; pp.18–19 Helen Sessions/Alamy; pp.26–27 ValeStock/Shutterstock; pp.30–31 Science History Images/Alamy; p.33 (bottom) Les Palenik/Shutterstock; p.35 Marcin Wichary; pp.36–37 Paul King/Alamy; all other images from iStock and/or Shutterstock.

Library of Congress Cataloging-in-Publication Data
Names: Stark, Kristy, author.
Title: Failure : business blunders / Kristy Stark.
Description: Huntington Beach, CA : Teacher Created Materials, [2019] | Includes index.
Identifiers: LCCN 2017056449 (print) | LCCN 2017058373 (ebook) | ISBN 9781425850081 (e-book) | ISBN 9781425850081 (pbk.)
Subjects: LCSH: Business failures--History--Juvenile literature.
Classification: LCC HG3761 (ebook) | LCC HG3761 .S825 2019 (print) | DDC 338.09--dc23
LC record available at https://lccn.loc.gov/2017056449

Teacher Created Materials

5301 Oceanus Drive
Huntington Beach, CA 92649-1030
www.tcmpub.com

ISBN 978-1-4258-5008-1

© 2019 Teacher Created Materials, Inc.
Printed in China
Nordica.062018.CA21800492

Table of Contents

New businesses are established each day, hoping to fill a need or a **niche**. Existing businesses, on the other hand, attempt to grow and keep up with the demands of **consumers**. Both **scenarios** demand that business owners take some amount of risk. Sometimes, those risks pay off by attracting new customers or **investors** and by increasing annual profits. Other times, the risks do not pay off, and a company or a product fails.

Many large companies and wealthy business owners have experienced failure. Warren Buffett is one of the richest people in the world. Despite being very successful, he has had many business failures during his career. He once explained, "I bought a company in the mid-'90s called Dexter Shoe and paid $400 million for it. And it went to zero. And I gave away about $400 million worth of…stock, which is probably now worth $400 billion. …I've made lots of dumb decisions. It's part of the game."

Billionaires of the World

As of 2017, the world had 2,043 billionaires! They are worth a combined total of $7.7 trillion. One trillion is a 1 followed by 12 zeros!

Frugal Billionaire

Despite being worth billions of dollars, Buffett is a very **frugal** man. He still lives in the house that he bought in 1958. He bought it for $31,500.

Driving Toward Failure

The automobile industry is one of the largest markets in the world. Over 70 million cars are sold each year.

Despite millions of cars being sold, car companies still have the potential for failure. People running these companies may make bad choices when it comes to car designs, or they may ask too high a price for a specific car model.

The Ford Motor Company is one of the world's most recognized names. Even though Ford paved the way for the auto industry, the company still has had some blunders throughout its history. Perhaps its biggest failure was the Ford Edsel.

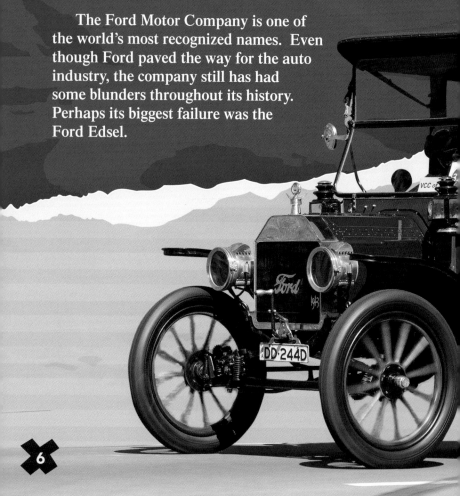

Ford's Top Seller

The top-selling cars in the United States are actually trucks. The Ford truck series ranks at the top of the list. Its F-series trucks include the F-150 and the F-250 models. A total of 820,000 F-series trucks were sold in 2016.

Ford's Model T

Ford introduced the Model T in 1908. It cost $850. Today, that would be around $22,000. The company sold 15 million Model T cars. It was one of the best-selling cars of all time.

Ford's History

Ford Motor Company was founded in 1903 by Henry Ford. He had designed and built cars for several years before founding the company. In 1913, he changed the automobile industry forever by creating the moving **assembly line**, which made it possible to produce cars at a much faster rate. What once took 12 hours now took 2 ½ hours.

THINK LINK

> How does Henry Ford's moving assembly line affect car companies today?

> Are consumers today affected by the assembly line? How?

> How did higher wages benefit Ford's employees? Describe ways that the high wages also benefited Ford.

Developing and Marketing the Edsel

In 1955, Ford began developing the Edsel. The company planned to design a car based on what consumers wanted. Designers sought the opinions of shoppers as they developed the car. In the end, they did not listen to what customers were saying. The people at Ford ignored the data from the polls and made the Edsel their way.

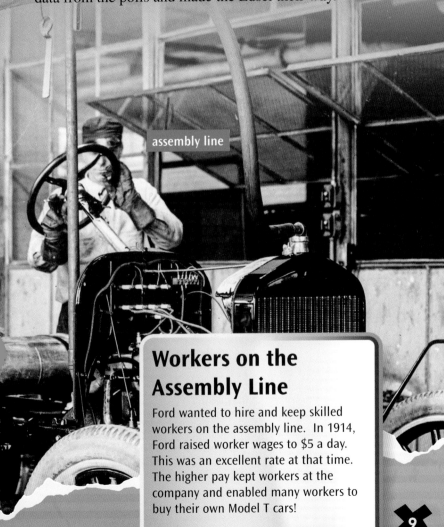

assembly line

Workers on the Assembly Line

Ford wanted to hire and keep skilled workers on the assembly line. In 1914, Ford raised worker wages to $5 a day. This was an excellent rate at that time. The higher pay kept workers at the company and enabled many workers to buy their own Model T cars!

Along with bad design, the Edsel could not live up to the hype. Ford's marketing department worked in overdrive, publicizing the car before its release date. The ads promised an **innovative** "car of the future." After a year's worth of ads about the "E-car," people lined up at car dealerships to see this new car. But people were disappointed when the Edsel was finally released on September 4, 1957. After all the hype, they expected something more exciting. Most people thought the car was ugly with a huge front **grille**.

That Huge Front Grille

Car shoppers did not like the look of the Edsel's gigantic front grille. But its large size had a purpose: to let air in and cool the engine.

No one, including employees and company executives, liked the name of the car. Edsel, the name of Ford's son, was quickly **dismissed** as a car name during the development process. However, after they considered thousands of possible names, company officials eventually settled on the name Edsel, even though it had been rejected earlier. Car shoppers did not think the name sounded like the car of the future. They thought it sounded boring.

Desperate for a Name

Ford asked poet Marianne Moore to submit names for the new car. Some of Moore's suggestions included "The Intelligent Whale," "The Silver Sword," and "Utopian Turtletop."

Rare Collector's Car

Because so few Edsels were produced, they are now worth a lot of money. An Edsel in good condition can sell for up to $47,000!

Not Worth the Price

The U.S. economy was in a **recession** when the Edsel was released. Because money was tight, people were careful about what they purchased. The price of the Edsel was a lot higher than other Ford models of the time. The starting price was $2,500, and the most expensive Edsel model cost $3,800. In today's dollars, this is a starting price of $21,000. People were not willing to pay the higher price, especially for a car that didn't look good.

Recession of 1958

During the recession, over five million people lost their jobs. That meant that almost 7 percent of the labor force was not working. Without jobs, people were not spending money on nonessential items, such as new cars.

End of the Edsel

The Ford Motor Company quickly realized that the Edsel was a mistake. It only made the car for two years. By the time Ford stopped making the Edsel in 1959, the company had lost an estimated $250 million. That is worth about $2 billion today! The Edsel proved to be a costly and embarrassing mistake.

Companies have learned from the mistakes made with the Edsel. Today, the name Edsel is **synonymous** with failure.

The Design Process: Success with Feedback

Ford asked for consumer feedback again—for its Sync 3®, which was released in 2016. This time, Ford listened to what people wanted. This system lets drivers control cars audio systems and make calls using only their voices. Ford designers used the following process for the new system:

Developers brainstormed ideas about what the system would do, and they used customers' feedback about the previous Sync systems.

Designers developed a prototype for consumers to test outside of a car. The testers answered questions about the system and reported any issues they encountered. This feedback was used to modify the system.

Designers mapped out the system to determine how users would get from one screen to the next. They thought about how to make it simple to navigate.

Designers tested the system on open roads, so they could see how it would function for drivers.

The product was released to consumers. When problems arise, Ford sends software updates to the system.

Testers used the system inside a car on a closed track. Designers observed the testers, while other employees sat in the cars to get feedback from drivers.

Some employees used and tested the product.

Going Flat

The Coca-Cola Company is one of the most well-known brands in the world. In fact, it is the world's largest beverage company. Its products are sold in more than two hundred countries. Over 100,000 people work for Coca-Cola.

But being famous doesn't mean that a brand is **immune** to failure. Like Ford, any thriving business can be one bad product away from losing a lot of money. Any company can head toward ruin because of one product flop. In the 1980s, Coca-Cola found itself in such a place. The company made one of the most epic mistakes in business history.

The first formula for Coca-Cola was made by John S. Pemberton in 1886. Soda fountains in **pharmacies** served the drink around the United States. Nine years later, the soda was sold in every state and U.S. territory.

Soda in Space

Coke and Pepsi became the first sodas to go to outer space. Astronauts on a space shuttle tested a special "Space Can" on their mission in July 1985. The can had to open in low gravity without spraying soda everywhere.

Tasty Fun

In China, Coca-Cola is called *kekou kele* (KUH-koh kuh-LUH). The name means tasty fun. The company came up with a Chinese name that sounds similar to its English name and shows the spirit of the brand.

Pepsi Challenge

Fierce Competition

By 1904, Coca-Cola sold more than one million gallons of Coke each year. Talk about a fast-growing business! As the company grew, a new **competitor** entered the soda market. In 1898, a **pharmacist** named Caleb Bradham invented Pepsi-Cola. It took a while for sales of the Pepsi-Cola Company (also known as PepsiCo) to increase, but it became Coke's biggest **rival**. And it still is.

Soda for Breakfast?

In 1989, PepsiCo released Pepsi A.M. This soda was a breakfast drink that had 28 percent more caffeine than regular Pepsi. The product was not successful, and Pepsi stopped selling it the following year.

In the 1980s, Pepsi sales began to affect Coke sales. By 1985, sales for both Coke and Pepsi were getting closer to each other. This change was due to Pepsi's clever marketing. Ads for Pepsi projected the image that the soda brand was for young people. A promotion called the "Pepsi Challenge" had a huge effect on sales, too. Participants in the challenge did a blind taste-test of the two sodas. More participants chose the sweeter Pepsi over Coke.

New Formula

The Coca-Cola Company fought to compete with PepsiCo. The company wanted to win over Pepsi drinkers. Since people liked the sweeter taste of Pepsi, Coke changed its formula. This had not happened in nearly one hundred years.

The company did a lot of research to make sure people would like the new formula. About 200,000 people tested the new drink. The company listened to feedback from the testers. It continued to change the mix based on what people said. Finally, it came up with a soda that the testers liked more than both Pepsi and the original Coke.

In April 1985, the Coca-Cola Company launched the new drink. After doing so much research, the company was satisfied with its product. Company leaders and employees were confident that people would love it.

Another Formula Change

In 2013, Coca-Cola Life launched in Argentina. This soda is sweetened with **stevia** and cane sugar instead of high-fructose corn syrup. It has 65 percent of the calories of regular Coke. The soda hit stores in the United States in 2014.

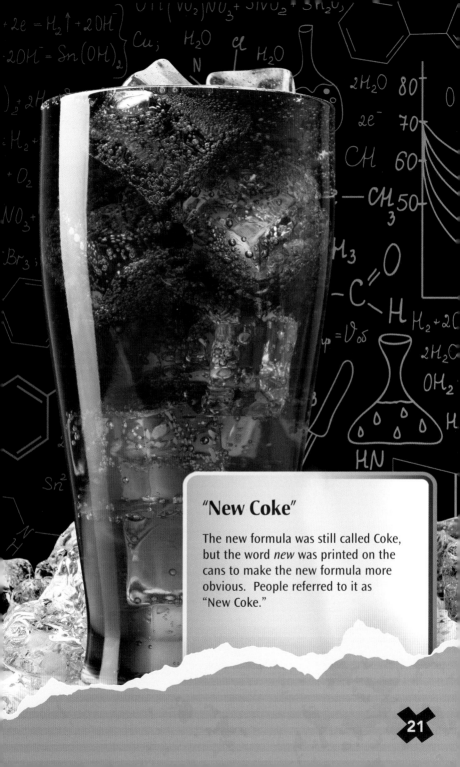

"New Coke"

The new formula was still called Coke, but the word *new* was printed on the cans to make the new formula more obvious. People referred to it as "New Coke."

The public hated the new formula! More than that, consumers were mad. Coca-Cola received about 400,000 angry phone calls and letters. People told the company how much they disliked the new product. They also begged Coca-Cola to bring back the "old" formula.

Coca-Cola soon realized that consumers are motivated by more than a soda's taste. The old formula and logo had been around for a long time, and many people bought Coke because it brought back memories for them. Some people bought Coke out of habit or **loyalty** to the brand. Even though many people chose Pepsi in the blind taste-tests, this didn't mean that they would stop buying the old Coke. And it didn't mean that they wanted the old formula to be replaced.

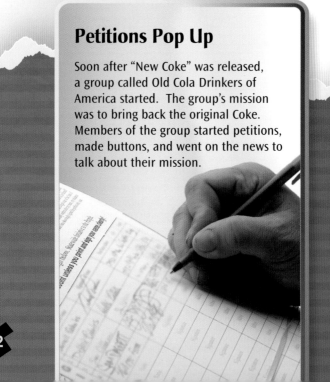

Petitions Pop Up

Soon after "New Coke" was released, a group called Old Cola Drinkers of America started. The group's mission was to bring back the original Coke. Members of the group started petitions, made buttons, and went on the news to talk about their mission.

Stocking Up

When the formula change was announced, some people bought extra cases of the original formula. Some people filled their basements with the soda. One man in Texas bought $1,000 worth of Coke.

Taking Action

Coca-Cola knew it needed to act quickly. The outcry against the new soda was strong. The company could not risk losing more customers to Pepsi.

In July 1985, the company's president announced that it would bring back the old formula. "New Coke" lasted only 77 days before it was officially cut from production. The old formula was re-released as "Coca-Cola Classic." This is the same formula that is used today.

It is safe to say that Coca-Cola learned its lesson about trying to change its **iconic** soda. The company also learned that its customers were loyal to the brand. At the same time, the company was able to take away attention from Pepsi.

Drinks Made by Coca-Cola

The Coca-Cola Company produces more than just Coke. It also makes many other beverages. These include Sprite, Minute Maid, Fanta, and Powerade.

This graph shows the Coca-Cola Company's annual sales from 2012 to 2016.

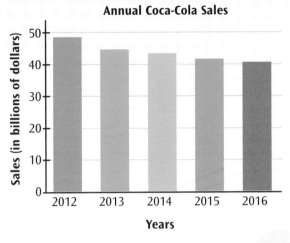

Annual Coca-Cola Sales

> In what year did the company have the highest sales? In what year did the company have the lowest sales?

> What do you think the sales trends in the graph mean for the company?

Billion-Dollar Business

The Coca-Cola Company recovered from its "New Coke" blunder. In 2016, its annual **revenue** was $41 billion.

Chip Failure

You have probably heard of Frito-Lay snacks. The company makes Lay's, Cheetos, and Ruffles chips as well as Cracker Jack, Sun Chips, Doritos, and many others. A snack company's main goal is to produce items that people love to eat. At one time, making tasty snacks was all that mattered.

History of Frito-Lay

In 1932, C. E. Doolin started the Frito Company. In the same year, Herman W. Lay started a chip business. Thirty years later, the two companies **merged** to form Frito-Lay Inc.

1.49

Sale
99¢
EFFECTIVE UNTIL SEP 20

1.49

Sale
99¢
SEP 20

Ingredients Galore

Frito-Lay has many products with a variety of ingredients. Its classic potato chips have only three ingredients. Its Doritos chips have over 25 ingredients!

But companies today often try to target people's desire to eat better and live healthier lives. They make snacks that have less fat and fewer calories.

Frito-Lay was one of the first companies that tried to make a healthier snack. It succeeded in creating a fat-free snack, but the chips were a disaster for the company and a painful experience for consumers.

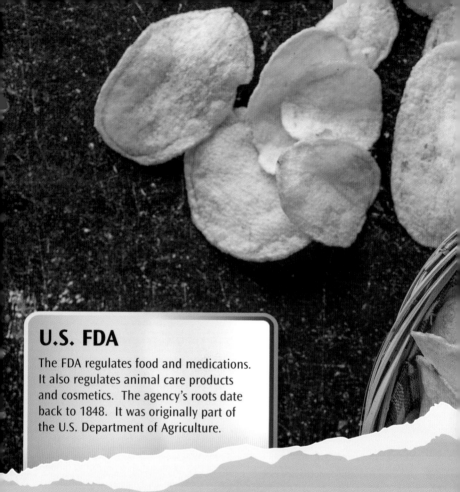

U.S. FDA

The FDA regulates food and medications. It also regulates animal care products and cosmetics. The agency's roots date back to 1848. It was originally part of the U.S. Department of Agriculture.

Olestra Pains

Frito-Lay wanted to add a snack brand that would appeal to **health-conscious** consumers. In 1996, the U.S. Food and Drug Administration (FDA) approved a food **additive** called olestra. Frito-Lay created a chip made with olestra. People thought that this **compound** could take the place of unhealthy oils and butter.

Eating Fake Fat

In 2011, researchers at Purdue University in Indiana conducted a study on rats. The rats were given either regular chips or chips made with fake fats. When rats ate the chips made with fake fats, they ate more and gained more weight than the other rats. Researchers believe that "fat substitutes can interfere with the body's ability to regulate what it eats, and that can result in overeating."

Frito-Lay was one of the first companies to make a snack using olestra. The company launched its line of WOW! potato chips in 1998. WOW! chips had no fat and only 75 calories per ounce. Compare this to regular chips of the time, which had about 10 grams of fat and 150 calories per ounce. It seemed that the company was offering consumers a healthier option.

Researchers and the FDA believed that olestra was safe, but since it was new to the market, no one anticipated how people's bodies would react to it. They thought that its fat-like taste with none of the fat-related health concerns would be a big benefit.

It turned out that olestra's **molecules** were too big for the body to digest. People's bodies could not break down or absorb olestra, so it passed through the body's digestive tract. This caused people to have painful stomach cramps and diarrhea. Eating WOW! chips was the equivalent of taking a **laxative**.

When word got out, people stopped buying the chips. Sales of the chips were about $400 million in 1998 but dropped to $200 million two years later.

Olestra Warnings

For a time, the FDA required a warning label on products with olestra. That requirement was lifted in 2003, and products no longer need the warning. Today, the FDA still considers olestra safe but only when certain vitamins are also added to the food.

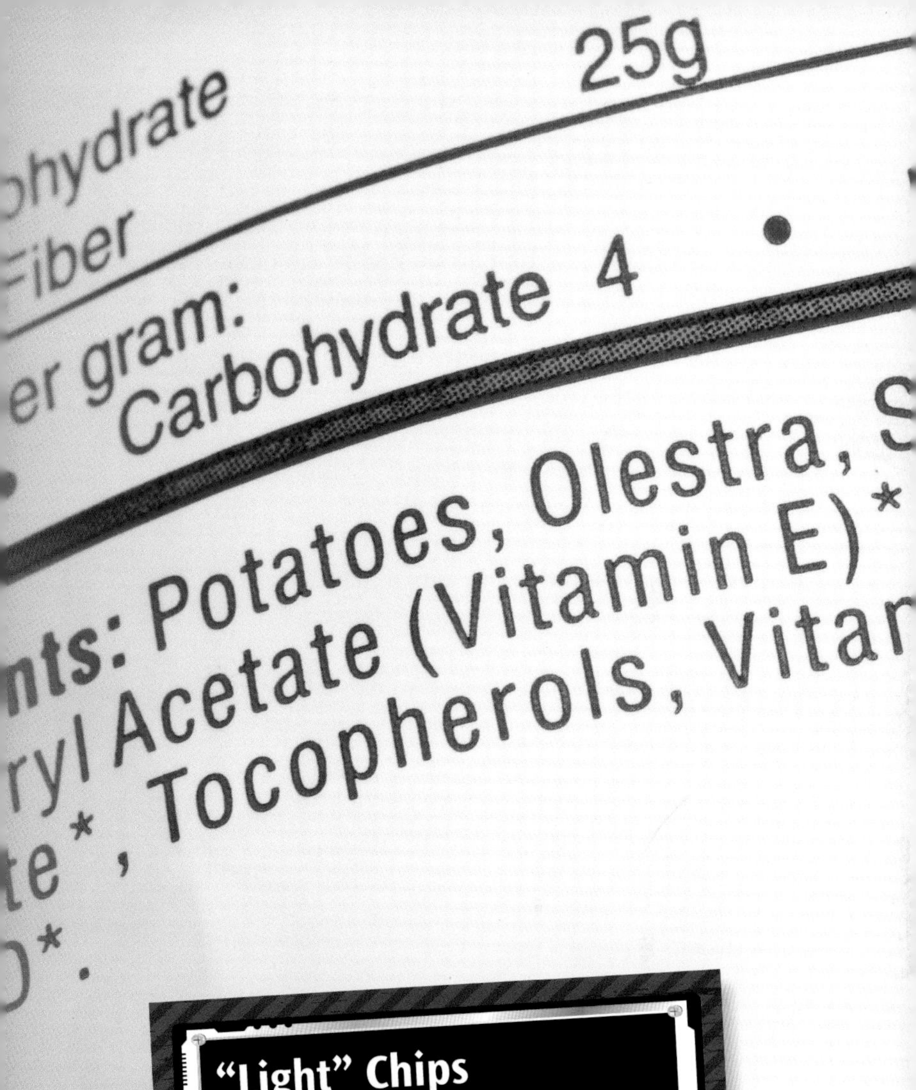

ohydrate

Fiber

er gram:

Carbohydrate 4

25g

Carbohydrate 4

nts: Potatoes, Olestra, S

ryl Acetate (Vitamin E)*

te*, Tocopherols, Vitar

O*.

ly ins

"Light" Chips

In 2004, "light" versions of some Lay's chips entered the market. These versions use olestra under the brand name Olean. They include more vitamins and no longer have warning labels about the chance of stomach cramps and diarrhea.

Tech Flop

Technology seems to change from one day to the next, so companies work hard to create the next best thing when it comes to devices and machines.

Technology that is now **obsolete** was once quite innovative for its time. Before Blu-ray and streaming services, the video cassette recorder (VCR) was used to watch movies and record TV shows. It used large cassette tapes to record and play video content. At the time, this technology was quite advanced. Sony led the way when the company released the Betamax machine in 1975.

VCR Wars

Soon after Sony released the Betamax machine, another company, JVC, released a similar machine. It was called Video Home System, or VHS. It was sold in Japan in 1976. VHS was released in the United States a year later.

First VHS Movies

The first film released to the public on VHS was a drama called *The Young Teacher*. It was released in South Korea in 1976. The first American films on VHS were *The Sound of Music*, *Patton*, and *M*A*S*H*.

VCR with VHS tapes

Sony Walkman

In 1979, Sony sold the first model of a personal stereo, called the Walkman. It played audio cassette tapes, and some models could play the radio. It was small enough to carry around and listen to with headphones. It became one of Sony's most popular products.

Both machines worked in a similar way, but the formats were not compatible. A Betamax tape would not work in a VHS player, and a VHS tape would not work in a Betamax machine.

The two companies were competing for the same customers. Soon, Sony began to lose the battle. When Sony made the Betamax, it hadn't considered certain factors. For example, Betamax machines cost a lot more than JVC's machines. Typically, when consumers have a choice between similar products, they will select the ones that cost less.

Betamax tapes had better picture resolution and better sound quality than VHS. However, better quality also meant that the Betamax tapes cost more than VHS. In addition to having a higher cost, the Betamax tapes could hold only one hour of content. The VHS tapes could hold two hours of video—about the length of a typical movie.

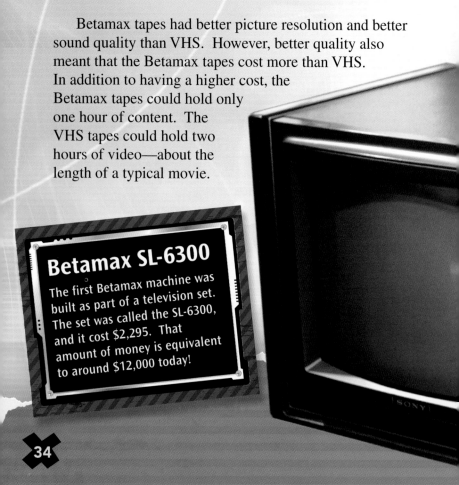

Betamax SL-6300

The first Betamax machine was built as part of a television set. The set was called the SL-6300, and it cost $2,295. That amount of money is equivalent to around $12,000 today!

Buy Your Own

The first stand-alone Betamax machine was the SL-7200. It cost around $1,300 when it was first sold. Today, you can find a **vintage** SL-7200 machine on eBay for around $100.

video rental store with VHS tapes

DRAMA

DVDs Hit the Market

Movies on DVD were first released in 1997. However, studios continued to release movies on VHS until 2006.

Perhaps Sony's biggest mistake was to keep the Betamax format **proprietary**. Other companies could not use the technology. On the other hand, JVC licensed its VHS format to other electronics companies. This meant that other brands of VHS machines were soon on the market. In 1977, the VHS format took 40 percent of the VCR market. Ten years later, 90 percent of the VCRs sold in the United States used the VHS format.

Long-Lasting Tech

In July 2016, the last VCR was produced. Funai Electric of Japan finally stopped making the machines. After 40 years as the leading format, VHS is nearly obsolete.

Because there were many more VHS machines on the market, movies and content were sold in VHS format. Long before Redbox and Netflix, **brick-and-mortar** video stores were lined with rows and rows of VHS tapes for people to rent. In fact, VHS remained the dominant format until DVDs took over in the early 2000s.

Knowing When to Quit

By the 1980s, it was obvious that most people preferred VHS to Betamax. When a company makes a failing product, it usually takes swift action to cut its losses and move on. But Sony did something rather surprising. It continued to make Betamax machines despite losing sales to the VHS format. They did not stop production and move on. In fact, Sony kept making Betamax machines until 2002.

People can only guess why Sony did this. Perhaps Sony thought the better quality would lure people back to its product eventually. Technology changed a lot in the following years. By the time Sony stopped producing Betamax, DVD players had already begun to replace VCRs.

Blu-ray vs. HD DVD

In the early 2000s, another format war took place—Sony's Blu-ray versus Toshiba's high-definition DVD format. This time, Sony was victorious. Blu-ray became the most available format for movies and games.

Betamax Tapes

Sony kept making Betamax tapes even after it stopped making the machines. In November 2015, Sony announced that it would stop producing the tapes in Japan. Sony made the tapes for 40 years despite all the problems and failures.

Learn from Failures

Many successful business owners and companies know that they will make mistakes. No matter how much research, time, and effort are put into a new business or product, there is still a chance that consumers will be unhappy. And if consumers do not like something, they will not buy it.

Business owners cannot predict the future, so they continue to take risks when they launch new products. Without taking risks, business owners might miss the chance to develop the next new tech gadget. The fear of failure might keep someone from investing in something that could change the world. Business owners learn to put fear aside and invest in good products. All businesses hope to avoid an Edsel or "New Coke" catastrophe!

Risking Failure

Steve Jobs, cofounder of Apple, knew that life and business involve taking risks and not worrying about failing. He once said, "The greatest artists like [Bob] Dylan, [Pablo] Picasso, and [Isaac] Newton risked failure. And if we want to be great, we've got to risk it, too."

Missed Opportunity

William Orton was the president of the Western Union Telegraph company. In the 1870s, Alexander Graham Bell offered to sell the patent for the telephone to Orton for $100,000. Orton declined the offer. He said, "Mr. Bell, after careful consideration of your invention…we have come to the conclusion it has no commercial possibilities.…What use could this company have for an electrical toy?"

Glossary

additive—a chemical or substance that is added in small amounts to another substance to improve it in some way

assembly line—a mechanical production process where work passes from one thing to the next in a line

brick-and-mortar—a store or business that is in a building instead of on the Internet

competitor—someone who is trying to succeed in business or sports

compound—something that is formed by combining two or more substances

consumers—people who buy goods and services

dismissed—decided not to think about or consider

frugal—careful about spending money or resources when you do not need to

grille—a metal frame that is used to cover or protect something

health-conscious—concerned about one's health and trying to eat healthy foods

iconic—widely known or recognized

immune—not affected by something

innovative—having new ideas about to do something

investors—people who give their money to businesses for shares in the businesses

laxative—a medicine that relieves constipation

loyalty—the state of being constant in support of someone or something

merged—joined together to make one company

molecules—the smallest possible amounts of a substance

niche—a place or job for which a person or a thing is best fitted

obsolete—no longer used because it has been replaced by something newer

pharmacies—stores where medicines are prepared and sold

pharmacist—a person whose job is to prepare and sell medicines that doctors prescribe for patients

proprietary—used, made, or sold only by the company that has the legal right to do so

recession—a time in which there is a decrease in economic activity and many people do not have jobs

revenue—money that is made by a business

rival—a person or company that tries to be more successful than another

scenarios—descriptions of what could possibly happen

stevia—a powder made from a plant, which is used as a zero-calorie sweetener

synonymous—very strongly associated with something

vintage—something that is not new but is valuable because of its good condition

Index

Check It Out!

Books

Allen, Frederick. 2015. *Secret Formula: The Inside Story of How Coca-Cola Became the Best-Known Brand in the World*. Open Road Media.

Carroll, Paul B., and Chunka Mui. 2009. *Billion Dollar Lessons: What You Can Learn from the Most Inexcusable Business Failures of the Last 25 Years*. Portfolio.

Mitchell, Barbara. 1986. *We'll Race You, Henry: A Story about Henry Ford*. Lerner Classroom.

Rogers, Sam. 2013. *Steve Jobs for Kids*. CreateSpace Independent Publishing Platform.

Videos

Hodge, Channon, and David Gillen. "Epic Fail, Business Edition." *New York Times*. www.nytimes.com.

"Betamax vs. VHS: How Sony Lost the Original Home Video Format War." *Gizmodo*. www.gizmodo.com.

Websites

Coca-Cola. www.coca-colacompany.com/#History.

Entrepreneur. www.entrepreneur.com/slideshow/219445.

Frito-Lay. www.fritolay.com/company.

Try It!

Imagine that you are creating a new product. Think about the steps you would take to make sure that your product does not fail.

- Ask people what products they would want to buy. What products would make their lives easier.

- Next, decide what product would best meet consumers' needs.

- Design a product based on the feedback you gathered. Draw an image that shows the product, and write a description about what the product can do.

- Present your product to an audience. Be sure to tell people about what the product does and how it will make their lives easier.

About the Author

Kristy Stark writes books about a variety of topics. She writes about everything from the history of telephones to the game of Quidditch. When she is not busy writing, she enjoys running, reading, and doing just about anything outdoors. Most of all, she loves to spend time with her husband and two young children. They love to go swimming, hiking, and camping in the warm California sun.